Vision Focused Life: Living Your Life with Extreme Purpose

JAY & ANNIE ADKINS

Table of Contents

Foreword

Life is a highway and on the road of life you will experience detours and roadblocks that attempt to slow you down. Those who make shifts and properly course correct are the ones who end up successfully at their desired destination. Those who allow the challenges of life to force them off the road will end up at a dead end that may ultimately lead to their demise.

Road maps were designed to help people navigate their way from point A to point B. In business, route guidance – a coach or mentor who can help you create a plan of action and an effective route to reach your goals – will enable you to enter the Express Lane to success.

When you take massive action combined with the right relationships, you will ignite an entire possibility unimagined by the average person.

If you want to go fast in life, go alone.

If you want to go far in life, go together.

Jay and Annie are the drivers you want to help you drive your chosen financial vehicle.

Jay and Annie have not only become great friends over the years but mentors who I look to as I continue to change lanes and accelerate my own dreams. Their hearts are paved with gold. Their souls are paved with wholesomeness. And they are faith-driven warriors which gives me the hope and trust that they will guide me in the right direction. They are genuinely selfless and their passion for others is the fuel that will assist you in becoming your own champion both personally and professionally.

This book is the ultimate guide to your best life.

If there was ever a time to follow your passion and do something that matters to you, that time is most certainly now.

It's your turn to make a shift and take your life into overdrive. It's time to put the pedal to the metal.

Don't let life pass you by. Bypass the good life on the way to your best life. Make a shift and take your life into overdrive. It's time to accelerate your dreams. You are a Lane Changer!

Lane Ethridge

Founder, Changing Lanes International

Jay-logue

"Persistence. Perfection. Patience. Power. Prioritize your passion. It keeps you sane."

— Criss Jami, *Killosophy*

Mission: Our main focus for writing this book is to share with others the importance of having a vision for your life, having coaches/mentors to hold you accountable, having a network of like minded people to help one another achieve the greatest success in both business and in life, and overcoming adversities and obstacles to create your best life.

What You Will Learn:

1. How to create a business that supports your life
2. How to make it your mission to help others succeed as well
3. Walk towards your fears to conquer them
4. Dream big
5. Always feed your mind with positivity—both information and people

6. Try new things professionally and personally

7. Stretch yourself beyond what you think is possible

8. Don't underestimate the power of others..... Be sure to join mastermind groups and hire coaches to help you get to where you want to go 10 times faster.

9. Track and review your progress regularly in all categories of your life.

10. You CAN make a decision to take massive action in your life, to overcome fears, obstacles trials and tribulations.

11. Have fun in all you do! And lead as many people as you can along the way

In an effort to share and relay these important concepts, we have gathered together a group of highly successful entrepreneurs from our network of colleagues and asked them to share their stories as well. We are all on a journey together through life, and it is our greatest hope that this collection of real life rock stars who have conquered and overcome the greatest of challenges will inspire you to do the same.

The Value of Mentorship

"Tell me and I forget, teach me and I may remember, involve me and I learn."

— Benjamin Franklin

If you talk to the majority of Americans today, they would tell you that they would love nothing more than to own their own business and be in control of their time. Unfortunately, most have absolutely no idea how to go about this, or even worse, the wrong idea. Though there is more than one way to approach entrepreneurship, there are definitely ways that will lead you down the wrong path rather quickly. Our goal with this book is to share our journey, so that our readers can benefit from our time and talents, but also learn from our mistakes and in turn avoid making the same ones themselves.

Throughout our journey, we have learned countless lessons with one of the most valuable being the importance of mentorship. Mentors and coaches are priceless in our professional lives and more importantly our personal lives and can not only guide us in the right direction, but also help us steer clear of obstacles that could slow us down.

In an entrepreneurial role, time is your most precious resource and most choose to mentor others instead of spending time on their own learning, But we contend that mentoring is vital in all aspects of your life, and we still have our coaches even though we also mentor others. Mentoring offers many things here are just a few key components:

- Perspective and Experience. A mentor can give you the benefit of his or her perspective and experience. He or she can help you assimilate to a new opportunity and give you an insider's view on how to get things done.

- Think Outside the Box. A mentor can help you look at situations in new ways. He or she can ask hard questions and help you solve problems.

- Define and Reach Long-Term Goals. A mentor can help you define your career path and ensure that you don't lose focus and continue down that road even when you become distracted by day-to-day pressures.

- Accountability. When you know you are meeting with your mentor, you ensure that all the tasks you discussed in your last meeting are completed. This helps prevent procrastination which ultimately leads to frustration and laziness.

- Trusted Coaches to Discuss Issues. A mentor can be a great sounding board for all issues – whether you are having difficulty with your customers, an ethical dilemma, or need advice on how to tackle a new project or move in a different direction.

- Champion and cheerleader. A mentor who knows you well can be a strong champion of your positive attributes and an ally during any bumpy spots in your career. As a mentee, it is important to build trust and prove yourself worthy. Mentors will encourage mentees to share their story and share themselves. It's hard to champion someone if you don't know who they are, which is why we spend a great deal of time getting to know our coaching students.

- Expand your contacts and network. A mentor can help expand your network of contacts and business acquaintances. A valuable network is about quality, not quantity. You want to surround yourself with people who will you grow and succeed.

- Open Doors. A mentor can open doors within their sphere of influence that can lead to extremely beneficial opportunities. Referrals are the life blood of most small businesses, and a mentor can assist in expanding your client base.

- Inspire. A mentor whose work you admire can be a strong inspiration, which is another reason we decided to write this book. We have a story to tell, and we hope it can inspire even just one person to believe in themselves and not give up, no matter how bleak the outlook appears.

- Work smarter. With the help of a good mentor, you can work more efficiently with a clearer view of the future you are trying to achieve. This helps you feel more confident in your role as a business owner, which leads to better performance and more success along your chosen road. Time management is so important as an entrepreneur, and your mentor or coach will help you keep a sustainable work/life balance so you can live the life of your choosing.

- Transitions- into new businesses or tweaking or rebuilding your existing business or businesses into one that works for you instead of you for it.

To get more information on what to ask a potential mentor/coach or to check out our mentoring program please visit
http://www.visionfocusedlife.com/coachingquestions

A Lesson in Persistence

"The harder you fall, the heavier your heart; the heavier your heart, the stronger you climb; the stronger you climb, the higher your pedestal."

— Criss Jami, *Killosophy*

The birth of a child is a joyous occasion marked by the overwhelming feeling of anticipation for a bright future. For us, the arrival of our middle daughter Jazmyn, added a warm and loving addition to our growing family. Jazmyn at first seemed to thrive as a baby, and was bright and curious as she grew as most toddlers are. But something was brewing beneath the surface of her eye and began to become visible by the time she reached the age of two.

A growth was forming underneath her skin and pushing on her right eye to the point of disfiguring her adorable face. After numerous examinations, biopsies and countless tests, doctors were still stumped, and sent off a sample of the growth to a specialized lab for analysis. At first it was thought to be neurofibromatosis, and her doctors argued over this diagnosis for over 6 years.

Finally, a genetics test was ordered and they discovered it was in fact a genetic mutation of the cells that is isolated to the area around her eye and right cheek called an "Isolated Plexiform Neurofibroma." This condition can possibly be fatal, and is for many if the disease is in the patient's genetic make-up because it can spread to other areas, and tends to attack organs but fortunately Jazmyn's is a spontaneous mutation and not present in her DNA.

The happy go lucky girl has endured 5 grueling surgeries so far to 'debulk' the growth and reconstruct her face. Doctors are always keeping a close watch on the tumor, as rapid growth is common as puberty approaches, Jazmyn is currently 11 and they want to ensure growth is kept under control as much as possible. This is a condition that would be devastating to most children and their families—but not our clan.

Many people have asked us "how do you do it?" All of the appointments, rescheduled surgeries, changes in plans and actions. We have always stayed positive and had the vision of a positive end result in our minds. Jazmyn asked her doctor what the overall plan and outcome would be when the process all began and he explained to her he plans on the right side matching the left side of her face when he is finished with the process, which in turn gave us all a plan and goal to have in our minds to achieve, and her doctor gave us a way to develop a plan to achieve that goal. For more information or updates on Jazmyn please visit www.jazmynscause.org

Adversity has long been weaved into our DNA, and we've learned to embrace it and use it as a tool to better ourselves and our children. We hope that through this book, you too will be able to see past the roadblocks that have been put in your path and ultimately live out your dream life. Tenacity and persistence are your friends, and no matter the obstacles, you can never give up on yourself—If you don't believe in you, who will?

Giving Up is Not an Option

"Nothing in this world can take the place of persistence. Talent will not; nothing is more common than unsuccessful men with talent. Genius will not; unrewarded genius is almost a proverb. Education will not; the world is full of educated derelicts. Persistence and determination alone are omnipotent. The slogan Press On! has solved and always will solve the problems of the human race."

— Calvin Coolidge

Our daughters' daunting medical challenges were not our first brush with adversity. We're a couple who has built a foundation of love and trust due to our steadfast dedication to not giving up despite the odds. Our story begins in high school choir—2 love-struck teenagers who beat the odds and marry after college. Jay is an accomplished vocalist, and his first foray into entrepreneurship was as a wedding DJ and singer. But we were no ordinary budding entrepreneurs. We were one of the first entertainment companies to have a website in central Ohio and were booked 4 to 5 weddings deep every weekend. Who'd have thought that something many would find a silly hobby would spark a fire in us both to be business owners?

But all was not well in our fairytale. As life progressed, so did Jay's drinking. This led to a blur of arguments, ultimatums, sleepless nights and hurtful exchanges. A void deep within Jay's soul was eating away at his relationships and his future. Instead of turning to God, he was turning to alcohol as so many often do.

Following our time at college, we married, both of us wanting bigger and better things for our lives, and in hopes that the drinking would get better and we could have a family. However the drinking did not improve, in fact it became worse. It had a hold over him that wouldn't let go. No matter how much I begged, pleaded, threatened or cajoled, Jay just couldn't seem to shake it. It owned him.

As a young and inexperienced twenty something, I had no idea the size of the beast she was up against. I thought the heavy drinking would subside once Jay grew up a little and had the responsibility of a family. My naiveté couldn't see Jay was a full blown alcoholic and not just someone who parties a little too hard. Because of this, I didn't realize that every time I grabbed a six pack of beer when I bought groceries I was in fact enabling an addict. My attempts at 'loving him' through it were failing miserably.

Rock Bottom Doesn't Have to be the End

"I think this is what we all want to hear: that we are not alone in hitting the bottom, and that it is possible to come out of that place courageous, beautiful, and strong."
— Anna White, *Mended: Thoughts on Life, Love, and Leaps of Faith*

Jay was struggling to balance his family and work life with the demands of his demons, and one night, the demons finally won. Jay spent the evening drinking heavily after work and got behind the wheel drunk, as he often did, only this time his luck ran out. Now facing a DUI and in jail, Jay thought this was rock bottom.

Even amidst the chaos of caring for 3 young children while my husband faced criminal charges, I felt a sense of relief. Maybe this would finally be the wake up call for Jay that I had been praying for. Surely, he could see that he had a problem that was taking over his life.

When Jay was released, he vowed he was done drinking and he was going to turn his life around. And for a time, he did. But most of us know that alcoholism is a vicious and vile disease that grabs a hold of people and doesn't let go. The change was temporary, and within months, Jay was back to drinking in full force.

I was at a loss. Jay's drinking had spiraled out of control and she didn't know how to convince him to do something about it. I had never felt so helpless in my entire life. I had the weight of the world on my shoulders and felt as if I just couldn't bear the burden any more. But Jay wasn't ready.

In the midst of the storm, Jay had begun to study real estate. He discovered he had a knack for buying low and selling high. We decided to upgrade their home to accommodate our growing family, so we leased out our current home and bought a bigger one. We discovered that the tenants' lease payments were covering their mortgage AND putting $250 in their pocket every month. We were hooked!

Several months later, I arrived home late in the evening after a long day at work to discover our 3 young children completely unsupervised and Jay unconscious from over imbibing. Something in me snapped. It was one thing to endanger his life with his drinking, but another one entirely to put our children at risk. I had never been so angry and hurt, and drew the line in the sand for Jay. Something had to change—I was done with the lies, excuses and undeserved rationalizations. He had a problem and he needed to handle it.

Jay stopped drinking successfully for the next 3 months, he was working hard and doing all he could to be present and involved, sober.

During that time we acquired 5 properties, some through lease option agreements and the business was flourishing, but the drinking intervened one last time.

I had to leave for a week of training for work and the kids were at my parents' house in Kentucky, Jay was a bachelor for the week and it was his downfall. After going out to dinner for a steak by himself, he began drinking and after numerous drinks he climbed back in the car and headed home, this time he fell asleep at the wheel and hit a tree head on. After running from the police, through a river and ultimately being tasered twice, Jay went to jail once again for a DUI. Once in court the judge gave Jay his changing ultimatum, go to rehab or go to prison for two years. Jay woke up the next morning and for the first time got on his knees and prayed to God to help him. At that one given moment he made a decision to change his life no matter what it would take. He entered inpatient rehab and was determined to beat the odds. In the 3 weeks he resided there, I discovered I was pregnant with our 4th child. This made Jay even more determined to succeed. He had a wife and a family who needed him, and he owed it to himself and to us to overcome this disease.

I had a full time job but it wasn't enough to cover all of their expenses, and once I announced that I was expecting our fourth child they decided I was "no longer a team player" and fired me.   We lost everything—our first home, our current home and our other properties.   We had no home, no money and no jobs—all with 3 young children under the age of 6 and another one on the way.

Outpatient rehab followed, and with the help of our family and friends and his renewed faith in God, Jay has been sober for 10 years this October.(2015)

Climbing out of the Abyss

"Each night, when I go to sleep, I die. And the next morning,
when I wake up, I am reborn."

— Mahatma Gandhi

O nce Jay had exited rehab, he tapped into an old acquaintance in real estate to help him buy a property that the family could live in while he fixed it up. This lease option turned into the break we needed. We were able to start over as real estate investors, private money lenders and mortgage brokers. There wasn't anything about real estate that we didn't touch. Jay and I immersed ourselves in learning anything and everything we could to ensure success.

But of course, life's curveballs weren't over. The crash of the real estate bubble gave birth to Senate Bill 185 which limited one's ability to be all things to all people in real estate. You could no longer be the mortgage lender and the real estate agent simultaneously—so I stepped in and got my Loan officer's license while Jay focused on the real estate side. Our teamwork was now taking shape outside of our home as well, we were excited about the possibilities!

With all of these great things beginning to happen in our lives, we met and reconnected with many people within the real estate realm, that were not only liked minded but vision focused as well. One of those people was Bob Bevard, who not only was Jay's high school English teacher, but someone who we wanted to collaborate more with. We actually decided between the three of us and a few other likeminded people to form a mastermind group, this group not only allowed us to bounce ideas off of each other for business, but it also helped us to hold each other accountable for goals that we often set.

Bob's Story

"Character consists of what you do on the third and fourth tries."

— James A. Michener

I am honored that one of my former students from my teaching career has invited me to participate in his (and his wife's) book. It has been a goal of mine to write about the amazing powers that lie within each of us and this invitation has prompted me to begin this worthwhile goal.

As an English teacher, I was at times able to lightly touch upon this subject, but never in much depth. There are so many ideas that the traditional school environment doesn't allow for. I have frequently thought of a course entitled, "all the things I couldn't teach you in high school." Perhaps this "assignment" will assist me in pursuing this idea.

Like many people, I came from a very dysfunctional family. As a result, my grade cards in school consisted of as many "D's an F's" as one could accumulate and still be passed on to the next grade. I often thought I was passed on so that teacher wouldn't get stuck with me two years in a row. Finally, in high school, after my parents were divorced and there was much less turmoil in my life, my experience in school began to improve.

Half way through my freshman year, my English teacher went on maternity leave and an exciting new teacher took her place. He made all of us feel like we were capable and that our opinions and ideas were important. He also became my wrestling coach the following year. His attitude, encouragement, and enthusiasm was an inspiration to me and all of the team members.

With success in wrestling, I began to believe that I could possibly become successful in other areas of life. I set out for college reading at about the eighth grade level and never having written even a simple "essay." My goal was to simply pass my freshman year. All of the classes I had taken in high school were "general track" courses except three. My junior year I took biology and Algebra one. My senior year, I took geometry. That was it. Through a lot of work (everything took me two or three times as much time as everyone else) I managed to succeed in that goal. It was during this time that I became interested in reading various kinds of "self-help, motivational, and spiritual" kinds of books. I realized that I had in fact internalized a tremendous amount of negative and self-limiting ways of thinking. I began practicing meditation and applying the technique of visualization to various areas of my life.

The biggest problem that I ran into was the world that surrounded me. Whenever I attempted to discuss some of the ideas presented in one of these books with a friend or family member, I found that I might as well have been talking about "Big Foot," ghosts, or alien visitations.

Because of this lack of support, my progress might best be described as two steps forward and one step backward. At times I was able to achieve some remarkable results in specific areas. However, sharing such experiences with someone was a sure way to find out that it was "purely coincidence, luck, or the result of simply working hard."

I have come to know that "Seek ye the kingdom of God first, and then all things shall be added unto you," is the one of the most misunderstood and yet powerful statements of the Bible. Whenever I heard this or certain other quotes from the Bible, I filtered it through the very narrow interpretation that I had obtained from going to church as a child. How about you? What thoughts do you have when you hear this quote? Perhaps you are of a different religion or you profess to not be a believer. My understanding of this statement is not from a denominational or "religious" point of view. I hope to share with you an understanding that will both empower and liberate you from some of the self-limiting beliefs that you may have about yourself and the world in which you live.

Perhaps I should share a few stories before proceeding. After teaching high school English for thirty years, I retired. Time for the rocking chair, right? Not exactly. At age fifty-four, I took up racing downhill mountain bikes. I had been mountain biking for about ten years, but downhill mountain biking is a totally different kind of sport. At times you are flying down the mountain at speeds in excess of 40 mph. You jump off of rocks as much as twelve to fifteen feet high, you do man built jumps as much as thirty feet long, you traverse through "rock gardens" with jagged boulders that could send you flying over the handle bars. All of this, on a bicycle.

During this time, most places that I raced did not have a 50 plus age group because very few riders were still racing downhill after the age of 50. I was often competing against guys who were fifteen years younger than me. I campaigned for such a category to be formed. IMBA (international mountain biking association) did have a 50 plus category, but most of the places that I raced in the eastern part of the U.S. didn't have this age group. By the time I retired from the sport (age 60) this category was added to many of the venues.

Visualization was a very powerful and important part of my success (and survival) in this sport. Often, when I would come to a new race course, there would be several features that were designed to separate the skill levels of the riders. You could choose to do the "go around," but that frequently meant that you wouldn't be in contention for placing in the race. I developed an important habit. I would look at a feature and decide:

1) is this within my ability range? Have I done a jump or drop almost this big in the past?

2) Can I visualize myself doing this feature successfully?

3) Next, I would practice it in my mind. I would see myself doing it correctly, then, once I decided to do it.

4) I would commit 100% with confidence and faith of doing it right.

This was crucial in this sport. Not completing it correctly could have meant very serious injury or even worse. If there were doubts lurking about, I wouldn't attempt the feature until I could clearly see myself successfully completing that feature. I can remember times prior to this habit where I allowed a doubt to come into my mind sometime during the attempt. The results were not good. I learned that there was no place for a negative thought in downhill racing.

As a fifty-eight-year-old, I qualified to compete in the Nationals. Along with two downhill friends, I headed to Sol Vista, Colorado to compete in the 50 plus downhill nationals. I told my two companions that I wasn't going out there to simply compete, I was going out there to win. There were many factors leading up to the day of the race, but one decision that I made was to eliminate jumping hard off of one of the jumps that I had been doing well in practice.

For my race run, I simply jumped off of it gently and then hammered the rest of the course. At the end of the run, I soon found that I had won the nationals. I over-heard one of the guys I was competing against say to his companion, "I had it sowed up! Then I came off of that one jump with the sharp turn right after it, and I crashed. I think I broke my leg, but I finished and still got second place."

Why did I decide to take that jump more gently? I just had a feeling; on a conscious level I did know that this section was becoming progressively more difficult the more it was being used, but it was just a feeling that lead me to this decision. How is it that I won a national championship in my first attempt to do so? Because I decided that I was going to win and I saw myself winning the event! In my meditations, I visualized myself having a perfect run on the day of the race. I was so convinced of it that when my buddies wanted to go to Keystone (a different downhill mountain biking park) the day before the race, I went with them. I gave up a day of practice, even though my habit was to practice the entire day before a race. Had I practiced and trained hard? Yes, but to clearly state that I was going to win and to see myself having that perfect run were significant parts of the end results.

Why have I chosen to tell you this story? I will be sixty-four by the time this book is published. I still barefoot water ski, ride dirt bikes, mountain bike, snow ski, stand on my hands, and in general, defy the cultural beliefs about aging. If I had listened to my friends and family, I would have " started acting my age" forty years earlier. I am so glad that I didn't. I am discussing sports because the principles that have made all the difference in my life can be applied to sports, business, health, relationships, or any area of your life.

By now, perhaps you have begun to realize that "seeking the kingdom of God first" to me, doesn't mean going to a monastery and giving up all of your worldly possessions and activities like I had once believed. It does mean that I take the time to quiet my mind and tap into the tremendous power that we have been given. It does mean we let go of the barrage of self-limiting and negative thoughts that we have internalized about ourselves. This is were the "work" comes into place. It isn't hard work, but it's simply outside of the habits that most of us grow up with.

Remember that I mentioned two steps forward and one backwards? Remember that I mentioned not applying the principles to all areas of my life? When it came to relationships my track record was not so great. After my second divorce, I was somewhat an emotional train wreck. I allowed myself to wallow in self pity. As such, what were my dominate thoughts about myself? Do you suppose that I was attracting the best person into my life? No, I was kicking myself around and so, I was attracting someone into my life who would also kick me around. You see, I still had some very negative beliefs about myself from my childhood. I believed that I was not truly worthy of a quality person. I believed that I needed to accept the first person who would have me. Guess what I got?

Seven years into the marriage (just long enough to qualify as a long term marriage in Ohio) my wife took me to cleaners in the most incredibly devastating fashion that I have ever seen or heard of. She was able to decimate me financially. Over half of what I had worked thirty years to achieve was simply given to her because she did such a remarkable job of making our finances seem completely co-mingled and confusing. It took six years to get through and $40,000 in lawyer fees, to lose beyond belief.

So, I was 59 years old, retired from teaching, and had been hoping I would be able to travel, ride bicycles, water ski, and basically live the good life. Much of my time and resources were wasted defending myself in this divorce. I had a choice. I could accept my financial status at the time and content myself with living a modest life, or I could start over. Really, at age 59, start over?

One of the most important things that I did immediately after the divorce proceedings began was to begin attending a group, called Celebrate Recovery. No, I didn't have a drug problem. I had issues with anger. My anger was the unpredictable hurricane that suddenly appeared from nowhere. As much as I had tried in every way to eradicate it, I had only been successful at temporarily postponing it. It was time to get healed and I was willing to try anything. I started going to counseling at the same time. I made healing my number one priority in life. Daily, in my meditations and prayers, I forgave all those who had abused/taken advantage of me. I attended these weekly sessions for four years. Getting freed from this demon freed me to move forward in all other areas of my life. If someone had told me that it was going to take four years, I probably wouldn't have done it. I was told that it would take about 18 months and this seemed reasonable. Once I started going; however, I saw the power of this healing process. If you have unresolved issues, you need to know that getting healed is the most important job that you will ever have. You can become extremely wealthy in one or two areas of your life, but it will never be true wealth. True wealth can only come to someone who has taken the time to be truly emotionally healed and healthy. Living a balanced life is what true wealth is really about. It includes your relationships, your emotional and physical health, your spiritual well being, and your financial success.

I decided not to date for two years so that I could truly focus on my healing. When I finally did start to date, I had a completely different attitude about what I was looking for and what I deserved. I began dating someone who was truly a kind hearted and genuine person. She was patient, kind, understanding, intelligent, and easy to get along with. Seven years later, I can honestly say that she is by far the best person I have every known. I attracted her into my life because I decided that I was worthy of someone of that caliber. I saw myself as being a very good person. I got rid of all of the buried pain and anger that had plagued much of my life.

Having peace with myself, and a quality relationship, gave me the strength to start rebuilding my finances, even though it didn't seem fair that I should have to do so after working so hard all of my life. What I have learned in the process, and I truly hope that YOU can learn this from me, is that "working hard" is not the key to success. The true key to success comes from within. The key to success is being at peace with yourself, forgiving yourself and all others, and deciding that becoming the best version of yourself is the best gift that you can give yourself and the world. Don't "get the cart before the horse." Take the time get your life truly in order. Take the time to learn about meditation and visualization. Believe that you truly can have an abundant life, not just the outside appearances of a good life. I know that this is the real key to happiness.

One of the beliefs that I have held for many years is that true intelligence is the ability to be happy. Someone can be a true genius in one area of life, but what good does it do him if he is not intelligent enough to be happy? How many times have you heard of someone who has all the signs of success and wealth, only to find that they are in fact miserable. They are addicted to drugs, alcohol, or simply are living miserable lives. What did you think when you heard that Robin Williams committed suicide? I was so sad. I loved his work, but on one level I was not shocked. Super success in one area of life, does not imply success in all areas of life. Our culture teaches us to glorify the sports heroes, the movie stars, the wealthy. Does our culture glorify having a balanced life? Do we talk about the person having a spiritual life? No, it's usually about who is at the top. It's usually about who has won or excelled in that one area. I gave you the example of winning the nationals for a reason. In our culture, this is one of the signs of "success." This is why I hesitate to discuss the next area with you. Please take into consideration that it is not more important than some other area of my life. It is more the result of having achieved a certain level of contentment and peace in the other areas of my life.

As stated, I was pretty much devastated by my ex-wife and the domestic courts. I then decided to see if I could improve my finances through real estate. One of my former students, who remembered that I was involved in real estate back when he was my student, called me to announce that he was a realtor and that if he could be of any assistance to me to let him know. That person, Jay Adkins, is the co-author of this book. We had talked about real estate before, but this time, I was ready to move forward. I started by seeing if I could re-finance my house. The payments were very high and took all of my retirement income to pay. Fortunately, I still had a modest income from my six-unit rental property that I had owned for about thirty-five years.

To my shock, even though I had a perfect credit score and track record for over 35 years, Chase turned down my request to simply go from a fifteen year loan to a thirty year loan. My payment literally would have gone to less than half, but they said that I couldn't afford this reduced payment! What? I can't afford this reduced payment, but it's okay for me to continue making the payment that I have never been late on and that is over twice as much? What kind of banking is that? I was really set back. I figured that I would not be able to move forward in real estate; however, I decided to search for another bank. This was in 2011 and the recovery from the recession had not begun. I was fortunate enough to find a mortgage broker who was able to refinance the house and even allow me to pull $30,000 of equity out of the house. My payments at that point were just over half of what I had been paying. The real clincher to this was that when the loan was sold on the secondary market, Chase is bank that purchased it! What does this tell you about big bank policies?

The good thing about this is that I had $30,000 to begin a new phase of real estate investing. I contacted

Jay and told him I needed a really inexpensive fixer-upper. It so happened that he had just bought one that he was going to flip for a quick profit. We worked out the price at twenty thousand and I was on my way. In the end, I had a total of $40,000 in the house. It appraised at $80,000 when I was done with it. Through many phone calls, I found a small bank that was willing to would work with me. They made me a loan for 80% of the appraised value. So, I put a renter in it at $825 a month. I walked away from the bank with $64,000 ($24,000 more than I put in it) and began looking for my next house. From there, in less than four years, I have purchased and remodeled 24 houses. The average house is around $120k, with a lake front property that appraised at 350k on the high end. I have kept and rented all of these houses and am now shifting into the selling phase of my business. My net worth basically quadrupled in less than four years and my monthly income tripled. Do I have any regrets about starting over? No, I have decided that I will probably be somewhat active in real estate for as long as I am able to do so. Can you imagine this 100 year old man saying, "I'm still buying and selling real estate all over the world!"

The success that I have had is directly a result of the small banks that were willing to finance me. I seem to have had much better luck than anyone that I know in doing so. I have been told by all of them that I do it better than anyone else that they know. One banker that recently told me they would be happy to continue to do a substantial amount of business with me, seriously suggested that I should be teaching others how to grow there business in real estate. I have learned so much about real estate in the past four years. But most importantly, I have applied the same concepts to real estate as I have to sports and other areas of my life. Most mornings, I take a half an hour to forty-five minutes to meditate. During this process, I reserve time to solve problems and visualize the end results that I am working towards. On the days that I rush out of the house without doing so, I find myself running in circles and accomplishing much less than I could have if I had only taken time to do this.

So, more important than teaching others about real estate, would be teaching others the concept of using the incredible power of their minds to create balanced lives. This is what true wealth is all about. True happiness comes from within. When you achieve that, the other things are "added unto thee" with ease, not hard work...

If you would like to learn more detail about any of the above mentioned subjects, you are welcome to email me at bobbevard1@yahoo.com. I am in the process of becoming certified as a life coach and have now decided to write my own book.

"How To Live Your Most Abundant Life Now"
Craig Fuhr a real estate investor, speaker, and mentor wrote an article titled this exact same thing. To paraphrase what he stated in this article: How would you define prosperity? It is defined by Webster as "the state of being successful usually by making a lot of money" Prosperity can mean many things to many

different people but if you were to sit and think about what the true meaning of prosperity was to you, it would probably depend on how you define success.

You are typically taught growing up that, success is measured by the "things" you own and the amount of money in your bank account. However, when older people who are in hospice care for their remaining time on earth are asked about their lives, never do they say "I wish I had more money", in fact most say quite the contrary. When asked about their lives, most say they wish they had more TIME, that their lives meant something, and that they helped people somehow along the way. Time is something that you can never get back no matter how hard you try, and it is something that most people in business don't seem to have enough of. As Jay and I started growing our businesses, I began to notice that Jay in particular had less and less time available away from work. He was successful but missing out on a lot of time with me and the kids. We were and are always looking for additional ideas and tools to help us grow, maximize our potential and streamline our businesses. One event Jay attended that is held annually in Ohio is the OREIA (Ohio Real Estate Investors Association) convention. It was at this particular convention in October 2013, that he was introduced to the concept of being a "Lifeonaire". He came back from the convention and was very excited! He had signed us both up to attend a 3-day event that was strictly all about Lifeonaire. I, being the slight skeptic listened but chalked it up to another "idea" that Jay had found but would probably go nowhere, Boy was I *wrong!* We attended the three day event in St Louis, mapped out our personal and business vision and our entire outlook on life and on business was changed forever. While we were there we signed up to be part of a top level coaching /mastermind group. This group follows the principles of Lifeonaire, which includes building your business around your life and teaches you how to live your life in line with your ultimate vision. One of our coaches for this group Chuck Baumann, has made a huge impact on both our personal and business lives. In fact there was such a huge impact that Jay's working hours went from 75-80 hours a week to 25-30 hours a week within a period of about 6 months. This occurred solely because of the abilities our coaches, Chuck and Jason had to analyze our business and breakdown our processes, our willingness to be coached and our abilities in taking massive action!

Chuck's Story (One of Our Life Coaches)

"The mind is not a vessel to be filled, but a fire to be kindled."

— Plutarch

The first question I ask someone when they offer me coaching services, is "Who Coaches You?" As a long time coach, Steven Covey facilitator and former member of the Army, I understand the value of coaches and of coaches themselves having coaches. There is no ceiling to the learning process and it is a constant and ongoing journey.

Coaching is an invaluable resource that will keep you on task and on focus. It 's so easy for life to get in the way and distract us from our true vision; divorce, death, illness, job transition, children and unexpected change all contribute to people getting off course.

A written vision is also important to your future success. Being able to visualize your goals and how you are going to achieve them brings them into reality.

They are no longer just thoughts and dreams—they are tangible and achievable ideas.

If you stray from your vision, as most do at some point, both your mentor and the fact that you have written it down, will help bring you back to center and get refocused. A mastermind group will also assist you with this as well.

Mastermind groups are designed to not only provide accountability, but also a free flowing set of ideas. These groups are great places to help make your vision crystal clear, get constructive criticism and spark thoughts and wisdom that wouldn't have occurred to you otherwise.

Once you have your vision set, you have to ask yourself why you want these things. Do you really understand what it is you're looking for? The 'why' is key to your success, and if you don't fully understand it, you aren't setting yourself up to win. If you only want to work 25hrs/week and travel one week a month, but want to make $300,000/year, then you need to be making $300/hr when you are working.

If you're in real estate investing and rehabs and you're putting in your own toilets, that doesn't pay $300/hr. This means you're not living your vision by definition. You have to design a business around your parameters, or you will never succeed. A lot of people focus on the dollars but never taken into consideration the amount of time they have to earn. Balance is all about earning at the right rate to achieve the life you want.

You have to decide what your life should look like, and then design your business around it, and NOT vice versa. So many people want to do the reverse and design a life to fit around the business, and this never works. You will be over worked and underpaid and never realize the vision you set out with. When you share your vision with your coach and mastermind group, you are surrounded by people who have done what you are trying to do, and they are there to lift you up and help get you to the other side. If they can do it, so can you.

The last item on my bucket list was to climb Mount Whitney, it had been on there for decades and it was finally going to come true. The entire trip I struggled with a sore throat and after many visits to many different doctors and specialist upon my return I finally got a diagnosis. It was far worse than a stubborn sore throat, it was in fact cancer. My doctor was a bit dumbfounded that I was so calm about the entire ordeal, but I realized in that moment that I wasn't worried about many of the things that most people are in that situation. I wasn't worried about my finances, my relationships, my career or any of the myriad of things that most people worry about when they hear that diagnosis.. I obviously needed to concentrate on my health while I went through the treatment process, but I knew I didn't have the 'normal' stresses of the average American that would aggravate and impede the healing process.

Five years prior I had hired a coach and joined a mastermind group. At the time, I wrote a version of the vision that is still fundamentally the same as the one that I have today. The difference is, when I wrote that one, each line of it was virtually impossible. I was drowning in debt, going through a terrible divorce, out of shape, overweight and depressed. I simply followed the process in front of me and wrote what I wanted my life to look like. Something magical happened over the next several years...everything I wrote began to come true. My debt went away, I got into shape. I rebuilt relationships and changed everything about my life.

When I say that a vision, coaching and a mastermind group saved my life, I am not exaggerating. I literally believe that the guy I was before those things would not have survived the ordeal that cancer treatment is. He would have simply given up. He didn't have the energy to face any additional challenges. He would have died.

But I wasn't that guy when I found out. I was a much improved version of my former self and I never had a doubt in my mind that I would make it. ,It was most definitely the hardest thing I'd ever been through but I knew I had to focus on getting well and nothing else and I knew that was possible because all the other important areas of my life had been taken care of. It was ok to be out of balance for a while, I could afford to do that

It's been a year since my last treatment, and I now have clean bill of health. I believe that the balance in my life that I had at the time of diagnosis helped me to be able to focus on my recovery without being distracted. There's no such thing as a perfect life—bad things happen to good people—but you can control certain areas of your life and do what you need to do to create and sustain wealth, both financially and personally.

I use my story to pull others up and support them through the tough times in life. That is my calling. I was born to coach, and I can't imagine doing anything else. I even did coaching calls from my chemo treatment sessions to reinforce my belief in NO EXCUSES. If I can conduct coaching calls from the chemo center at the cancer clinics, then you can make time to take back your life—TODAY.

Renewed Hope

After joining the Lifeonaire family and coaching group, Jay and I had a new outlook on life and on business. We began to see where we could make adjustments to our businesses and ultimately gain larger strides in our lives. During this new awakening for us we began to interact with a lot of likeminded and motivated people, one of the couples in our coaching group are Aricka and Jonathan Brazer. These two are from the St Louis area and have a lot of great things happening within their lives and business. They too see the importance of having time together and with family, having a coach and overall accountability.

Aricka & Jonathan's Story

"Unless commitment is made, there are only promises and hopes; but no plans."

— Peter F. Drucker

In December 2013, Jonathan and Aricka Brazer heard on the radio about a free real estate course at a local hotel. It was through Rich Dad Poor Dad. At the event the Brazers were inspired to take a three day boot camp where they were encouraged to join local real estate clubs to build their network, dream team and knowledge. Jonathan and Aricka are the type that follow a blueprint, so that is what they did.

In January 2014 they attended and joined their first real estate investment club. It was called Lifeonaire. They didn't really get the name at first but were encouraged to read the book and got invited to the 3 day "Get a Life" boot camp. There, they were able to learn that they needed to build their business around the life they wanted to live. Aricka was working as a dental assistant full time and Jonathan was salesman for a home remodel company. They realized that the 9 to 5 J.O.B. (just over broke) wasn't the life they wanted. Jonathan was working seventy plus hours every week and Aricka was starting to have neck and wrist problems. So they decided to try something new. Aricka quit her job, and started a real estate business full time. That road was not smoothly paved.

The shift to a home based business proved to be more stressful on their relationship than what they anticipated. They learned quickly that they had very different communication skills. They started resenting each other. Jonathan was expecting faster results and clarity on what had been accomplished each day. Aricka barely even understood what she was supposed to be doing. Their relationship suffered as a result, and both began to wonder if this was really going to work.

When they went to the boot camp in January, they decided to join a high level coaching group that was offered. At a retreat that they had, with the help of their coaches in Lifeonaire, and other couples like Jay and Annie, Jonathan was able to realize the immense pressures he was placing on Aricka. The group was able to help him realize that he was jeopardizing what was most important to him. This shift led them to be able to not only repair their relationship, but allowed their new business to flourish.

The defined their visions and wrote their debt on a whiteboard and begin taking massive action and paying off their debt. They tried different areas of real estate investing. The Brazers wholesaled properties, kept some properties as rentals and even a rehab. They earned well on all of those different areas of real estate investing, but in August of 2014 they learned about lease options, control without ownership . This became their favorite niche of real estate investing. They have now paid off over $200,000.00 in debt and have taken more vacations than ever.

In order to do this, they have automated their business and hired virtual assistants to help carry the load. They have built a business that serves them, instead of a business that they serve. They found something that they are passionate about, and copied the blueprint of those that had gone before them. There's no point in reinventing the wheel—if it works for others, it will work for you.

They have affirmations on their bathroom mirror reminding them of their vision and what the Lord has planned for them. One of these is "We are successful real estate investors and proud of it." This reaffirms their beliefs that even if they're in a slow season they can't get hung up on that. They take action and go for it, no matter the circumstances. This is a daily challenge that Jonathan and Aricka face head on, and these affirmations help them to continue to take action regardless of our current state of affairs.

Because of this mindset and their dedication to their vision, they were able to work less and make more. They actually bought their current residence as a lease option. A beautiful turn-of-the-century farmhouse on 10.5 acres with 3 other residences on the land that pays for their mortgage. They have a handsome baby boy named Myles that came along after the stress was lifted. They do not regret any of the struggles and any choices that they made along the way. They have begun to successfully mentor others in business and life coaching. You can find out more about them at www.brazercouple.com

Associating With Like Minded People:

Through Lifeonaire, we have met a lot of different people, some involved in real estate, some involved in other entrepreneurial things and some just simply looking to better their lives and find a way to make things work for them instead of working for someone else. Part of the Lifeonaire vision is to help other people achieve their dreams and reach their goals. The best way to obtain this vision is by offering a coaching/ mastermind group to those that are interested in bettering themselves, believe that they can be coached and determined to make things happen. This group of individuals consists of several different coaching groups but all under the same lifeonaire principles. We have grown so much from the lifeonaire journey that not only do we maintain our spots within our own coaching group but now we too are coaches within the Lifeonaire family. Throughout the year Lifeonaire has several retreats where all of these individual coaching groups come together for at the very least one day to network, get reacquainted and simply to hang out. It is during one of these retreats that Jay and I met our wonderful friends, and now colleagues Keith and Shannon French and this is their story.

Keith & Shannon's Story

"Success doesn't come to you; you go to it."

— T. Scott McLeod

During 2005, Keith and Shannon were miserable in most every way. They were in jobs that paid well, but were unfulfilling, marriages that were failing and with families their jobs barely allowed time to have any interaction. They were collective pressure cookers ready to blow. Keith had traveled so much for work (over 50 countries), his frequent travel points total was a whopping *11 million.* As glamorous as this may sound, it's a life that eventually leads to burn out and discontentment.

Unbeknownst to the two of them, Keith and Shannon had worked for the same Fortune 100 company, though in different capacities, and were experiencing similar trials and tribulations. Both were going through divorces and dissatisfied with corporate America. Serendipity brought them together in 2006 at a real estate investing seminar in Atlanta, and in that moment, both of their lives were forever changed.

It was a classic case of love at first sight, and they knew they were soul mates. Just to try to convey how destiny works, here's a list of their crazy coincidences:

1. Worked for the same Fortune 100 company, but at different times and cities

2. Quit their respective corporate jobs for good within 13 days of each other

3. Started down the entrepreneurial path at the same time, both in real estate investing

4. Dissolved their first marriages at or around the same time

5. Attended several of the same real estate training seminars, but never crossed paths

Keith and Shannon decided to launch head first into their new real estate business ventures with the same passion as they did their personal relationship. Though their intentions were good, their approach was flawed. They grew too fast and borrowed too much, and when the real estate market crashed, so did they.

During 2008 to early 2009, they watched everything they had worked for disappear right before their eyes. Keith and Shannon were so broke, they snuck into hotels in the morning to eat breakfast at the free buffet, as their $40/mo grocery bill didn't allow for eating on a daily basis. They were staring rock bottom squarely in the eyes. Then came Lifeonaire.

They were invited to a Lifeonaire retreat, that thanks to Keith's miles, they were able to fly and stay for free so they could attend. They packed their bags with 25 cent cans of tuna and pudding cups so they could eat while they were there, and off they went. (On a side note, TSA thought the tuna was suspicious and put them through additional screening and the bomb scanner. And apparently those pudding cups are 4oz instead of 3oz and qualify as liquids, so they were promptly confiscated.)

At the retreat, their eyes were forever opened. Keith and Shannon realized they had never had a peer group that was positively focused, and a source of inspiration. They were able to share their journey without fear of judgment.

The biggest piece of wisdom that the group was adamant about, was that they needed to stop working at 8pm at night to start with, and then continue to trim that down even more. They were killing themselves working 18hr days trying to rebuild, and the Lifeonaire group realized this early on. That was the first step to getting their lives back, and was the turning point for them both.

It only took them about one and a half years to get their lives back on track. During 2009, they implemented their newly written vision, and during

2010 they got married, and began achieving things they never before thought possible. Their story of getting married on Bell Rock in Sedona, a vortex, at 4:44 pm on 4/4 (I guess they have something for 4's!) is inspiring. Every day they tell each other happy anniversary at 4:44 pm, no matter where they are.

They now run multiple successful online and offline businesses, and were able to restart and rebuild once again. Even in the depths of despair, they never blamed each other. Instead, they clung to the magic of their relationship and held each other up in the face of adversity. When the chips were down, they were each other's rock, and this has led to over a decade of love, happiness and success.

During their period of recovery, Keith and Shannon were able to refocus on life, by writing out their Visions and getting extreme clarity of their WHY. They were able to develop income streams that were derived from their true passions, which fit their newly designed lifestyles, and were no longer doing things they disliked as driven from a reactionary state of mere survival. No longer was money the impetus for existence, but life itself. They knew now, that they could do anything they wanted, and how to overcome limiting beliefs.

As part of their new life structure, they had to figure out how to operate their existing real estate business from anywhere they wanted to live, and not be bound by geographic constraints. A major driving factor was to be closer to Keith's aging mother, who lived alone 1200 miles away. They did not want to just see her one to two times per year anymore, but to be there with her and for her.

Not only did they figure out how to operate a successful remote real estate business and make the 1200 mile interstate move, but also throughout their brainstorming process they designed their own real estate investing strategy, Link Options, and began teaching others their unique niche strategy (www.LinkOptions.net), and support 100s of students nationwide. The purpose of their strategy is to help homeowners maximize their equity, and help tenant-buyers leave the rent world and become homeowners themselves. A delightful byproduct is helping communities maintain, if not maximize, their home values.

Today, Keith and Shannon are serial entrepreneurs and self-development mentors. They love sharing their life experiences and journey with their clients, and helping others overcome any barriers that may be keeping them from living the life of their dreams. This involves doing a thorough gap analysis on each person's situation – where they are currently as compared to where they want to be in both life and business, and then helping them close that gap.

They find it's amazing what a group of like-minded trusting peers (they call them kindred spirits) can achieve together, and how much fun it is to help others realize their life vision and to get clarity on their WHY. Also, they have other streams of income they thoroughly enjoy. Serendipity and divine blessings continue to grace them both.

Most recently, they have joined H9 Water (www.drinkH3O2.com), a network marketing company, during its start-up phase. They are pioneering closely with the founders, and are having a blast! Keith and Shannon believe this unique product is truly disruptive technology that has unfathomable potential to propel health and wellness to a whole new era in our generation.

To find out more about these two, their real estate training and coaching, life and business coaching, and other amazing products and services, go to their main website at www.KeithandShannonFrench.com.

Take Massive Action:
Throughout this book, I am sure you have noticed a common theme. Dream big, set goals and take action! The difference between people who want to be successful and people who are successful is mainly one

thing, successful people take massive action! While building out our businesses we decided to make things as simple and streamlined as possible. In our search for programs and other things that would help us do this, Jay came across a great software program that not only helps to do this but does so much more than we even initially realized. The software owner was a guy named Damon Remy, little did we know at the time of finding this program we would become great friends and have so much in common.

Damon's Story

"Don't ever give up. Don't ever give in. Don't ever stop trying. Don't ever sell out. And if you find yourself succumbing to one of the above for a brief moment, pick yourself up, brush yourself off, whisper a prayer, and start where you left off. But never, ever, ever give up."
— *Richelle E. Goodrich, Eena, The Tempter's Snare*

In 2008, I'd created a solid place for myself in the mortgage industry and was writing close to 100+ loans a month. Focusing on niches, one of which was Real Estate Investors, I'd locked into a specific high volume clientele and felt completely secure.

We were writing 100+ loans a month because, unlike our competitors, we had created software tools to help solve our client's issues around finding and closing deals.

We gave those tools away for free because we knew that if we helped Real Estate Investors do more deals, they'd need more money and they'd come to us to write the loans. And it worked great, for a while.

Then the housing bubble burst, and the financial markets tightened and banks put the screws on loan options I was able to offer my clients.

Just like that, I went from earning 6 figures a year to only $17,000 - dipping below the poverty level for my growing family. Our first son was 4 years old, my new baby girl was 4 months old, and my biggest concern became figuring out how to put food on the table.

Losing all security so quickly felt like a punch to the gut, and I was terrified. But, as they say, necessity is the mother of invention, and my family needed a solution fast. We were forced into bankruptcy and were facing foreclosure. Bouncing around rock bottom, I knew something needed to change.

So I started looking at all the software tools we'd created to help our Real Estate Investor clients in their businesses – tools that I'd been giving away for free. Our clients had been able to do so many deals because of the tools we'd provided, and even though the lending landscape had changed, the tools still worked, and Real Estate Investors, well they are a creative bunch and found alternative strategies to private finance their deals. I knew I had to monetize the software tools to support my family!

But I felt paralyzed by self-pity, the solution felt far off, and I couldn't take action because moving in any direction petrified me. Then, working late one night at the office, I stumbled upon a Tony Robbins YouTube video that flipped a switch in me. I'd never been into the self-help scene, and was quick to dismiss it, but there was something about this particular video that grabbed me – and thank God I listened.

In the video Tony drew 4 boxes – potential, action, result, and belief. He went on to say that we all have unlimited potential, but so few fully tap into it because of doubt and fear. When you have doubt, you don't take as much action as you should, which produces fewer results, diminishes your belief in yourself and decreases your perceived potential. It's an ongoing cycle and is why the poor get poorer and conversely why those with absolute certainty succeed.

I mean, think about that for a minute. If you knew beyond the shadow of a doubt, that you would succeed, how much action do you take on that great idea you have? Of course, you take massive action, you burn the ships. Retreat is easy if you have the option! We all hold on to something that serves as our safety net...our "just in case..." If you are not absolutely certain your actions are just shallow attempts never designed to succeed.

Something broke free for me during that fifteen minute video and I realized that if I didn't burn the ships, I would continue to cycle downward and I would take my family with me – and that's not something I was willing to do.

At that moment, I decided to relinquish my fear and take whatever action necessary to rebuild our lives. Racing home, I burst into our bedroom at 2am and woke my wife to share what I'd just learned. Though she thought I was half nuts, she humored me.

We had a full length mirror hanging on the wall, and I just happen to have a purple dry erase marker in my pocket, so I did my best to replicate the "4 Boxes" Tony had so eloquently used to convince me that anything was possible so long as I believed with certainty and took massive action! As I was finished I simply wrote…

We have to believe. We have to be certain.

When I'd finished, my wife turned to me and said, "I've believed in you all along. I still do. Now, you just have to believe in yourself."

That was a defining moment in my life and my business.

Over the coming months, I transformed my thinking and my business and created REI BlackBook, a software for real estate investors.

REI BlackBook automates many of the mundane activities that real estate investors have to perform, but, instead of buying and managing several different programs as they used to do, we rolled it into one.

What I'd found is most real estate investors struggle keenly with marketing and technology. They try to copy big companies, especially when it comes to marketing and get caught up in branding, which isn't what makes the little guy money.

Branding is all about you, when your focus should be on the customer. What's important is highlighting the actual solution for the individual you're targeting.

Your customers are sitting at home facing foreclosure and completely stressed out, desperately looking for someone who can help. I know, I've been there. Hence the Tony Robbins YouTube videos at midnight on a Tuesday.

Customers are seeking a solution, not a brand. It's not about building a brand, it's about solving problems. I knew that if I could create something that helped real estate investors market easily and effectively without taking a ton of time, they would succeed. And they have.

I've gone from being raised by a single mom on welfare, to six figures in the mortgage industry, to losing it all through bankruptcy, to rebuilding it all over again. REI BlackBook now stands to generate well into 7 figures this year, and that would never have been possible if I had allowed my fears to overpower my potential.

I still have that mirror and look at those statements in purple everyday. I've never erased it and never will.

You have to believe. You have to be certain.

Success doesn't happen to you; it comes with hard work, persistence, tenacity and a willingness to do whatever it takes. But I know for sure that if you're willing to move forward, if you're willing to never give up, success will happen for you.

One of my biggest passions in life to assist others in achieving their greatest success. To get you started I'm gifting you a free training on the 4 Building Blocks of Business. These videos and worksheets will give you a step by step guide to building a marketing funnel that brings the right kind of leads through your door.

This training has set thousands of student on the path to success; I know it will do the same for you.

Because, honestly, it's time to stop chasing the dream, and start living it. Get instant access by visiting: http://www.reiblackbook.com/gift-visionfocusedlife

Feed your Mind with Positive Ideas and Positive People

"The trouble is if you don't spend your life yourself, other people spend it for you."

— Peter Shaffer, *Five Finger Exercise: A Play*

One of the things that we as humans often do, is allow other people to control the outcome of our lives. The result of this, is we end up living lives we hate and piling that misery on to those around us. This leads to dissatisfaction professionally and personally. How many people have you met in your life that are a constant stream of complaints? If these are your circle of friends, then bow out of that circle post haste. Like attracts like, and you will never get out of the rut you are in if you surround yourself with those who have no desire but to whine about the hand in life they've been dealt.

Though human beings like to fancy themselves counselors and dispensers of wise advice, one thing we have learned in all of our years of mentorship is that a negative person will ultimately prevail in bringing you down—you will never bring them up. Surrounding yourself with positive people and positive environments will make a world of difference in your life.

Walk Towards Your Fears, Not Away From Them

Fear is a sneaky beast that creeps up on all of us when we least expect it, and sets up shop in every crevice of our minds. IT IS THE ENEMY OF SUCCESS. If left unchecked, fear will conquer every dream and every aspiration you've ever had, and prevent you from living the life you are meant to live. Fear is a natural response to the unknown, and should be embraced and used as a catalyst for change.

Geoffrey James, Contributing Editor at Inc. Magazine suggests these 4 mental tricks to conquer fear that we have found work brilliantly:

Value Courage Over Security

Repeated surveys have shown that most people value "security" over just about everything else in their lives. People will put up with jobs that they hate, marriages that make them miserable, and habits that are killing them (think "comfort food") simply to feel more secure.

To conquer fear, you must consciously dethrone "security" as the thing that you value most in your life and replace it with the active virtue of "courage." You must decide, once and for all, that it's more important for you to have the courage to do what you must to succeed, rather than to cling to the things that make you feel safe.

Differentiate Between Fear & Prudence

Most fears are irrational and unreasonable. For example, you might be afraid to make an important call because if the call doesn't go well, you'll have to face the fact that you "failed." Or you might be afraid to confront a co-worker who acts like a bully, or to start your own business because you're not certain you've got what it takes.

It's these irrational fears that hold you back and keep you from being more successful. That said, there are other kinds of fear that are actually just simple prudence. For example, you might be afraid to drive aggressively because you might cause an accident.

Prudence is a good thing. Just make sure you aren't pretending to be prudent--when you're just trying to avoid taking reasonable business risks, for instance, or putting yourself on the line to do what's necessary.

Treat Fear as a Call to Action

If what you fear is outside of your control (like an economic downturn), write down a specific plan of the exact steps that you'll take in order to adapt, if and when it happens. Once you've completed that task, put the plan aside and have the courage to forget about it. You've done what you can; it's time to move on.

But if what you fear is inside your control--some action that you're afraid to take, that is--take a few moments to prepare yourself, then do the thing that's scaring you.

We mean *now*. Not tomorrow; not next week. Right now, *before you read the rest of this book*. Call that person. Write that email. Create a business plan. Do it now!

Reframe Fear Into Excitement

Finally, tune in to the aspect of fear that's really fun. Think about the last time you rode a roller coaster: You probably felt plenty of fear, but you were also having a great time.

Let's face it, a life without fear--and without the courage to overcome fear--would be pretty bland and insipid.

Dream Big

When talking about dreams, it's hard to find a better (or bigger) example than Steve Jobs. He is a prime example of someone who dreamed bigger than anyone ever thought possible, and NEVER GAVE UP on that dream. Though sadly he is no longer her to continue sharing his wisdom, he did address the keys to Dreaming Big before his passing in an interview with Forbes magazine in 2010 as he believed that a compelling vision is one that inspires everyone's best efforts and meets these four criteria:

Big dreams are bold. Nobody is inspired by your goal to grow sales by 10 percent. Your team, employees, and partners are inspired by a vision that creates meaning in their lives and for the lives of your customers. In the mid 1970s personal computers were relegated to hobbyists. Steve Jobs' vision of putting a computer in the hands of everyday people was big, bold, and intoxicating.

Big dreams are specific. In 1961 John F. Kennedy inspired a nation by proposing a big idea and attaching a deadline to it. He said, "This nation should commit itself, before this decade is out, of landing a man on the moon and returning him safely to earth." Many scientists thought it could not be done but since Kennedy had set a deadline, they were forced to try. The conversation changed from "we can't do it" to "well, if we were to do it by the deadline, how would we accomplish it?"

Big dreams are concise. A big dream means little if it cannot be remembered. If Twitter had been around in the 60s, Kennedy's vision could have easily fit in a Twitter post! That's concise, and memorable.

Big dreams are consistent. Rarely are ideas commercialized without an inspired team of creative and passionate evangelists who turn that dream into a reality.

COMMUNICATE BIG DREAMS!

Build a Business That Supports Your Life—and Support Others Along the Way

So many of us have fallen into the trap of building a life that supports our business instead of building a business that supports our life. This minor tweak in thinking will make all the difference in the amount of joy and success we reap from our lives. Author, PJ McClure asks when addressing this issue: *"Would you take your family, jump into the middle of the ocean, and then try to build a boat around everyone? "* That seems ludicrous, right? But all too common in the business of life. When you're an entrepreneur, you don't have a personal life and a professional life—you just have a life. And that life should harmonize your family and your profession.

It's a myth that these are two separate entities— WIPE THAT FROM YOUR MIND! All you have to do is ask yourself one simple question:

"What do you want your life to look like?"

Once you can answer that question, you can begin looking at your business and deciding what fits and what doesn't.

In your quest to build an empire, don't be the one who buries their head in sand and pays no mind to those around them. One of the best things you can do for yourself and your business is to prop up those around you striving to do the same thing. Seeing others succeed is one of life's greatest joys, and will bring you a sense of satisfaction you could not otherwise achieve.

Experience New Things & Stretch Yourself Beyond Your Wildest Imaginings

Why do we resist stretching ourselves beyond our current boundaries when real living is just on the other side? We all do it, and fear is usually the culprit.

Here are some of the most common reasons we've found that this occurs both in ourselves and our coaching students:

- We fear the unknown. It might be worse than what we have now.

- We fear failure and looking bad in the eyes of others.

- We fear success. It will require more of us.

- We have limiting beliefs about what we "should" do and can do.

- We don't believe we are deserving.

- We don't want to offend other people.

- We can't or won't imagine how truly amazing life could be.

- We think it will require resources we don't have.

- We don't like discomfort.

Whatever it is that you hope might happen in the future won't happen unless you are doing something about it right in this very moment.

Living outside of your comfort zone doesn't mean you have to become someone you aren't. However, it does mean shifting up to the next level. Some stretches might move you forward a little, and some might propel you into an entirely new arena. Both are good. All forward movement is good. The key is to just do it! Don't sit around waiting for something to happen in your life—you have to make it happen, Take MASSIVE action!

Never Underestimate the Power of Mentors and Masterminds

Finding a mentor is helpful at any stage in your life, but especially for entrepreneurs. The question is, "How and where do you find a willing industry pro to mentor you?"

Answer: Anywhere!

Everybody could benefit from the helpful **guidance of a mentor**. Whether you're searching for a successful entrepreneur to bounce ideas off of or simply looking for someone open to sharing general business advice, it's never a bad idea to widen the scope of your current network by directly seeking out those you admire professionally. The question is, "How do you make their acquaintance in the first place?" The Entrepreneurial Council and we suggest trying one or more of the following:

1. ***Don't be just another face in the crowd.*** If someone you admire is scheduled to speak at an event or conference near you, you're in luck. But before you attend, do your research. Find out as much as you can about the talk's focus. Take steps to learn more about the topic so that you're

fully prepared to ask an intelligent question during the Q&A portion of the event. If it feels natural, consider lingering afterward for a post-presentation chat. Do be conscious of your potential mentor's time, though; let them leave if they're eyeing the door. Afterward, solidify the connection by paying a visit to their most-frequented social network and thank them or possibly add depth to your earlier discussion.

2. ***Meet up with a mission by networking actively.*** Joining a networking group can be painful if nobody in the group is in a line of work remotely similar to your own, or if—as is often the case—most of the attendees are as green as you are. That's why you need to try out a bunch of different groups before you settle on one or two. Websites like Meetup.com and Eventbrite.com are great places to start. When you find yourself surrounded by people who are smarter than you—or who are at least more experienced—then you know you're in the right place. Once

you've done that, make it your mission to talk to the one or two most interesting people in the room and exchange business cards with them.

3. *Get engaged—online.* Seek out business professionals who make good use of their blog, Facebook page or Twitter account. If your mentor-to-be shows lots of activity online, there's a chance they'll be open to interacting with you, at least virtually. Try to find two to three voices in your industry who truly inspire you. Then it's simple; subscribe to their feeds and read what they write. Once you know more about them, get ready to engage them. You want to catch your prospective mentor's attention, but not bother, or worse, bore them. Therefore, find an opportunity to provide value. If they pose questions or hold contests, that's your cue to jump in. If they're looking for recommendations for great iPhone app developers and you happen to know the best, get that information to them quickly. Keep your eye out for patterns: Perhaps

your would-be-mentor answers @replies on Twitter but rarely responds to Facebook comments, or always gets back to blog-post feedback but isn't so speedy when managing email correspondence with strangers (including you). Don't get discouraged when a reply isn't received. Decide which medium works best.

4. *Be ready to meet your mentor whenever or wherever.* By this, we mean be open to **chance meetings**. Stop wearing sweats to the airport, brush your hair before hitting the farmers market, and file your nails before that midnight movie. Sometimes, the most random encounters can and have turned into budding business relationships.

Track and Review Your Progress

When developing your strategy for setting goals and tracking progress, it's essential to find the core and constantly ask whether the strategy and the goals that lead to accomplishing that strategy relate to the core.

In their book *Made to Stick,* Chip and Dan Heath relate the story of how when a Southwest Airlines executive was questioned about why Southwest didn't serve food on their flights, the executive responded that adding meals would not help Southwest be the low-cost air carrier. Being the low-cost air carrier is Southwest's core; anything that diverts from that core is to be avoided. Keeping this idea clear in your mind as well as your vision acts as a very effective filter when determining goals and business plans. This step alone will aid you in accomplishing goals. It's far better to have a small amount of very focused and germane goals than it is to have a laundry list of random acts of improvement.

An important additional step in setting goals is to be certain that, as Jim Collins says in his world renowned book *Good to Great,* you confront the brutal truth without losing faith that you will succeed. Business is both full of challenges and full of opportunity. When setting goals, you must be certain to examine both. Too often entrepreneurs see the opportunity, but fail to accurately assess the challenges. Don't fall into this category. Instead, be sure to create goals in a manner where you face your challenges head-on. Again, as with avoiding random acts of improvement, facing the truth and developing strategies will enable you to maximize opportunity filters and focus your goals.

In terms of more specific strategy for accomplishing these goals once set, you should—of course—be certain that any short-term goals align with your long-term strategy. More specifically, your goals should have the following characteristics, they should be:

- Difficult but achievable
- Observable and measurable
- Specific, with a target date and/or the exact amount of money needed to the penny.
- Participatively set, when possible

In terms of tracking your goals, once they've been created using the principles above, again you must remember to confront the brutal truth. Resist the temptation to hedge on your evaluations of the efficacy of your progress. For instance, if you had a goal to draw 100 people to a webinar, and you got 50, it's important to attempt to figure out why you didn't hit your goal. Only by assessing the outcome of your goals by tracking them, can you continue to evolve your strategy. Over time, you begin to gather data which enables you to revise your strategies and achieve your goals.

In terms of specific goal tracking mechanisms, there are quite a few tools available for free online. Basecamp is a wonderful tool for creating a list of goals, and keeping track of progress. Similarly, Google Docs is a very good way to list a series of goals that can be shared by all parties involved. You can also visit our website www.visionfocusedlife.com to download a goal tracking tool that we personally use.

Good strategies evolve over time via an ongoing process of iteration and analysis. Remember, while you cannot measure and track your way to business excellence, you can certainly increase your odds of success.

And Most Importantly, Have Fun!

Sometimes we can get so focused and busy on the journey we don't realize we are running on empty in other area's of our lives. Unmet needs will eventually find a way of being met in unhealthy means unless we are aware and manage them well. Having fun is vitally important in stress management and living victoriously.

Studies show such wonderful health and stress relief benefits to laughter and even the anticipation of laughter, we should all work on getting more giggles into each day. Because of the many wellness benefits of leisure time, having fun should be a priority in the life of anyone who wants better health, greater happiness and less stress.

Stress management expert, Elizabeth Scott, M.S. offers these solutions to help each of us embrace FUN in our lives:

Have Friends Over More Often

Most people find themselves very busy these days — often busier than they want to be. While the activities that occupy our time are important, having fun is equally important. While busy lifestyles can sap us of our spontaneity, having friends over and setting aside some time just to play can offer a regular outlet for having fun. Worried that your house is too messy to have people over? There are simple and stress-relieving methods for cleaning, and you'll likely find that less clutter leads to less stress anyway.

Be 'In The Now'

There's currently a lot said in the media on mindfulness and "being in the now," and for good reason. When you're basing yourself firmly in the present moment (rather than ruminating on past or anticipated stressors), you're more open to happiness, laughter and having fun.

Maintain a Sense of Humor

You can turn your stresses into fun with an attitude shift if you focus on **maintaining a sense of humor in your daily life.** With a lighthearted attitude, events that would normally be annoying become amusing; big hassles become humorously absurd; major stressors become really great stories waiting to be told. Having a sense of humor is a big part of having fun — it's a way to actively seek out fun and happiness instead of waiting for it to come to you.

The biggest thing we have recognized as something we and others don't do enough of is to …

Celebrate The Small Stuff

You need to remember that not ALL of your goals are going to be met 100% of the time, but it is important to celebrate, even if just a little bit the accomplishments you do achieve. Too often it is easier to focus on the negative and the things you fell short on but it is crucial for your energy, your attitude and overall success to take time to celebrate every step along the way.

"In all of living, have much fun and laughter. Life is to be enjoyed, not just endured."

— Gordon B. Hinckley

Epilogue

We hope that in taking this journey with us, you have found a source of inspiration and hope as you travel down your own path towards success in life and in business. If you take nothing else from this book, take this: You have but ONE life, and your business should support that life and not vice versa. There are no mulligans or do-overs, we only have a set amount of time and no one knows when yours is up! So embrace your talents and passions to create a life you actually want to live, and have a blast along the way.

If we can do it, so can you!

About the Authors

Jay & Annie Adkins

Jay and Annie started their real estate career by simply renting out their personal home when they purchased a bigger home for their family in 2004, while building his experiences with the real estate market jay decided he would like to help others meet their real estate needs as well, so he decided to become a real estate agent and has been a successful hardworking one for over 8 yrs. While working with buyers and sellers jay saw how important it was to offer non conventional financing for those who have had less then perfect credit and where typical banks would not finance their homes. Based on this information jay and Annie both went to classes and obtained their mortgage licenses. Several years and countless experiences later, jay and another business partner opened a mortgage company to help in other ways with the home buying process.

Throughout the years Jay and Annie have met several people interested in getting into the real estate investment business but didn't know where to start, so together with some of those people, they created multiple LLC's and have developed a thriving real estate businesses with a total of 30+ houses that are either rented, rent to own, or already leased optioned, in addition to buying fixing and selling multiple houses per month. They have passionately mentored multiple people assisting them in building real estate portfolios in the millions. They also employ multiple people in the local community to rehab the homes that they and the people they mentor have purchased. They own several companies in the entertainment business as well and employ around a dozen people in that industry.

Although they are very passionate about real estate, they are even more so about helping others. They have developed a non profit that helps children with medical needs that are not covered by insurance companies, and enjoy seeing the reaction of parents as well as kids when they receive something they have been needing to help better their lives for so long! Check out www.jazmynscause.org for more information.

The most joy Jay and Annie receive, other then from their 4 children and their personal life together, is from helping others make their way in life and business through accomplishing their visions by using their coaching, mentoring and mastermind groups at www.visionfocusedlife.com. They receive great satisfaction when someone they are coaching goes through the vision and life development process allowing them to accomplish their goals 10x faster than the average person, whether that be people just starting out as a new investor or helping seasoned investors automate their businesses for the ultimate goal...or someone trying to transition into a new business to achieve time and money freedom. They both thoroughly enjoy their business as real estate investors and building their real estate profile and business one house at a time!

Based on this enjoyment and their love for life and helping others, Jay and Annie have an ultimate goal of giving back and helping others fulfill their visions.

Chuck Bauman

Chuck Bauman is an author, speaker, entrepreneur and Lifeonaire. He coaches many successful business people and has helped thousands of people to live their visions now rather than later. He has more certifications that will fit in a bio but mostly he knows how to get results. Results that allow people to grow their businesses in a way that creates more free time for the business owners to focus on the truly important aspects of their lives as defined by them.

Chuck is a decorated combat veteran, a cancer survivor and a one of the principle voices of Lifeonaire. His insight and wisdom make him one of the most sought after coaches in the arena today and his ability to cut thru all the propaganda and break things down to their essence is legendary among those he works with.

Keith and Shannon French

Keith and Shannon have been full time entrepreneurs since 2005, and offer real estate, business, and life coaching to experienced and aspiring entrepreneurs. They have also enjoyed speaking and training for audiences of all sizes. Since 2009, they have coached and trained hundreds of people on their unique real estate strategy that helped them survive the market crash.

Keith and Shannon specialize in helping people identify and monetize their passions. Some of their favorite businesses include internet marketing, real estate investing, network marketing and coaching.

In their downtime you'll find Keith and Shannon traveling and exploring places, hanging out at vineyards, hiking, and playing with their chow chow puppies and rescue kitties.

You can connect with them about their various businesses on their main website at www.KeithandShannonFrench.com or email them at info@KeithandShannonFrench.com.

Bob Brevard

Bob was born in Newark, Ohio in 1951. At thirteen he and his brother were the laborers for building their new house out in the country, and saw for the first time how a house was built and the sequence of doing so.

He graduated from high school in 1969 from Ohio University in 1976 and then moved back to Newark. Bob began teaching high school English and did so for the majority of his 30 career. He is always focused on helping students break out of their own self-limiting ways of thinking in order to achieve their true potential. Towards the end of his teaching career he was also a teacher mentor and a literacy coordinator.

Bob bought his first rental property the summer before he began teaching, and within two years owned 10 apartments. He obtained his real estate license in 1978, and sold real estate part time while teaching, remodeling apartments and managing his rental business.

His entire adult life has also included being involved in physical fitness and sports, such as racing dirt bikes, water skiing at a very high level, snow skiing, racing mountain bikes, etc. He is still doing most of those things to this day. He won the nationals in downhill mountain biking six years running in the 50+ class. Bob and his friend won first place in a mountain biking enduro this spring and were the oldest team out there—they were not split into age groups for this event.

At age 64, he is in the process of writing a biography, has five companies pertaining to remodeling, renting, and selling houses, and once his book is complete, his goal is to become a certified life coach.

Damon Remy

For more than two decades, Damon has made a home for himself on the leading edge of technology. Utilizing the Internet since the dial up days of yore, he continues to create progressive systems that allow companies to operate faster, more effectively, and more profitably!

Damon began his technology career in the US Marine Corps. Hand selected by his commanding general, he played an integral role in scouting, evaluating, and implementing the latest, most advanced technologies. At the time the technologies he utilized, such as IP video conferencing and logistical management systems - commonplace in today's market - were groundbreaking and cutting edge, even to the government.

After his military career, Damon's true nature as tech geek and digital entrepreneur emerged as he consulted with several companies, using technology to streamline and innovate their processes from the ground up. He renewed the operational effervescence of one of the nation's oldest Pepsi distributers through the complete revitalization of their internal systems.

In 2001, the world of real estate opened its arms to Damon, offering him a place as a consultant with a fast growing mortgage company that focused on real estate investors. In that rapidly expanding high-speed market, Damon developed systems for management workflow, lead tracking, and total business automation that skyrocketed many of his Loan Officers to national production rankings.

It was there in the trenches of the booming mortgage market that the concept for REI BlackBook was born. It's mission: work more effectively, productively, and profitably by simplifying in-house operations. In 2009, after several years of testing, a beta group of REI BlackBook users began seeing exceptional results, leading to the initial public launch and record day 1 sales. Today, REI BlackBook is the software of choice for leading real estate investors and the recommended platform by the nation's #1 Real Estate Education Company.

Jonathan & Aricka Brazer

Jonathan and Aricka Brazer are successful real estate investors in St Louis MO and surrounding areas. They have been part of Lifeonaire since January 2014 writing, updating, and changing their vision and focusing on paying down debt and becoming financially free. They started at over $200,000.00 in debt and have quickly shrunk it down to under $20,000.00. Without a vision they could not have achieved the things they have accomplished.

The Brazer's attend Apostolic Pentecostal Church in Mehlville, MO and have one son, Myles.

They are one of the only couples in the region that do Lease Options. They work successfully as couple to help many people learn how to achieve an abundant life and how to write and use a vision to get to the life they are looking for.

The Brazer's are currently investing and are developing a coaching program to help coach others to success. Spots are limited in the program so make sure you check out www.brazercouple.com to sign up.

www.ingramcontent.com/pod-product-compliance
Lightning Source LLC
LaVergne TN
LVHW021522080426
835509LV00018B/2620